How to Overcome Fear and Anxiety Forever: Definitive Guide to Conquer Your Fears and Enjoy Life to the Fullest

Dr. Lucas Allen

www.ingramcontent.com/pod-product-compliance
Lightning Source LLC
Chambersburg PA
CBHW061631130726
47996CB00003B/1227

Mit einem neuen Schwung in seinem Schritt schloss sich Erwin den jungen Elefanten in ihren Spielen an. Sie spielten Fangen, jagten Schmetterlingen nach und plantschten sogar in einem nahegelegenen Bach. Erwin lachte und scherzte mit seinen neuen Freunden, fühlte sich glücklicher und gesünder als seit Tagen.

Als die Sonne langsam unterging und lange Schatten über die Savanne warf, wurde Erwin klar, dass er zwar krank gewesen sein mochte, aber er immer noch der gleiche fröhliche Elefant war, der er immer gewesen war. Ein kleiner Schnupfen würde ihn nicht davon abhalten, das Leben in vollen Zügen zu genießen.

Mit einem zufriedenen Seufzer verabschiedete sich Erwin von seinen neuen Freunden und machte sich auf den Weg zurück in sein gemütliches Nest unter dem Affenbrotbaum. Als er sich für die Nacht niederließ, spürte er eine tiefe Dankbarkeit in sich - für seine Freunde, für Doktor Ellies klugen Rat und für die Schönheit der Welt um ihn herum.

Und während er einschlief, sein Rüssel noch immer von den Resten seiner Erkältung kitzelte, konnte Erwin nicht anders, als zu lächeln. Schließlich konnte selbst ein schniefender Elefant noch Freude an den einfachen Freuden des Lebens finden.

Table of Contents

" Anything that man gains must pay dearly, even if it is only with the fear of losing it."

Friedrich [1]Hebbel[2]

---

1. https://proverbia.net/autor/frases-de-friedrich-hebbel

2. https://proverbia.net/autor/frases-de-friedrich-hebbel

Prologue _

Do you feel like anxiety and fear are destroying your life? If so, I invite you to stay and finish this book, which will be your first step to overcoming your anxiety and fear.

Since always, we have all had anxiety to a greater or lesser extent. In such a way that the mild or intense sensations of that emotion have, to some extent, a beneficial effect because they supply us with better performance in certain activities that we carry out due to the emotion and attention they provoke. However, it should be noted that when it gets out of control, from mild to chronic, it can lead to a significant deterioration in our quality of life, and often with disastrous consequences... such as drug abuse, medication problems, marital, work, social problems, and as a last resort; suicide. And obviously, not to mention the great suffering experienced by the individual who suffers from this disorder.

My goal in writing this short book is to present, in an enjoyable way, the problem of this condition, and the ways to overcome, control, or eliminate it. To do this, I have based it on my own experience and the techniques and treatments that I used. The guide includes examples and exercises that will facilitate your understanding and assimilation of the main concepts. All the procedures described in the book have been proven to be effective against anxiety and fear if carried out as described... I'm not going to sell you smoke and tell you that this is pure magic: no! But if you put in effort every day and do exactly what I present here, you could control or incredibly improve your fears or anxiety. I invite you to enjoy the reading; the first step towards your healing. Thank you very much.

Author's note

The information and the exposed techniques should be taken solely as informative material for the person who suffers from this disorder... Nor should this guide be taken to replace the diagnosis and treatment of a specialist.

Introduction

Have you ever felt the following symptoms?

- racing heartbeat
- muscle aches
- Nausea in social situations
- Unexplained sweating
- vertigo, dizziness
- Shaking chills
- Shame it's not normal
- excessive worry
- Strange, repetitive, overflowing thoughts
- baseless fears
- Fear of dying of a sudden heart attack
- Need to check things or obsessively wash your hands
- Chills and shortness of breath
- choking

If you have answered **Yes** for the majority; This guide can be very useful for you, beyond 'healing yourself as if by magic' it can be a watershed for your healing, because you will know more thoroughly how it works. Anxiety and fears can manifest themselves in a wide range of ways. An anxious individual with fear or anxiety can feel tachycardia, fear in social situations (surrounded by people), catastrophic thoughts about the future, and even avoid places that can cause fear.

Some of the most common symptoms of this problem are constant mood swings, tremors, repeated doubts, panic. Some people who have this problem may present sudden anxiety episodes when they encounter triggers such as traveling by plane, the dark, or a certain animal. While other people just have constant anxiety without anything apparently triggering it.

In the hectic life in which we currently live, millions suffer from this disease. Some specialists maintain that at least five out of ten are or will suffer from anxiety symptoms in the coming years. While other studies carried out by the WHO, affirm that of every 3 men at least 6 women have had or will have moderate to chronic anxiety at some point in their lives.

The consequences of suffering from this generalized disorder can be many. Added to the discomfort it causes . Many times this is complicated by pictures of depression, drug abuse, and alcohol. And in others it prevents them from achieving a good job performance, finishing a career or knowing love... Fortunately, today, psychiatrists have many treatments and techniques that could help people who suffer from these ailments.

This guide tries to synthesize in an entertaining and orderly way all this already proven practical knowledge in an effective and simple way. It is without a doubt a book that could be very helpful at this time, if you find yourself mired in anxiety and fear. Nor do I want to tell you that you will achieve it in a week, but it can help you greatly if you apply all the knowledge exposed here to the letter. You may be wondering, but is it really possible to overcome fear and anxiety? Well, let me answer you honestly with a resounding YES... as long as you do everything your specialist recommends to the letter and as a second option what I expose in this book. If you do, you will start to feel much better and may even heal. Just to mention an example, there are more chances that you who suffer from fear and anxiety will be cured in months than a person who suffers from addictions or psychotic symptoms will. Therefore, if it is achieved in the end after having done your best, and it makes you feel better; I will be able to say with pride that this book has fulfilled its objective, and it has been worth it.

The correct way to overcome anxiety usually has eight phases, a list that you will read below :

- Understanding the disorder that causes anxiety
- Know in depth all the symptoms suffered by the anxious person (specifically those that are not so well known)
- Identify the specific form of how it presented itself in your life
- Make an analysis and select the most effective method, treatment or techniques to deal with it
- Learn said method or technique
- Apply them with discipline daily
- Evaluate the result
- And if it works, keep the stability

Anxiety - Understanding the disorder

Anxiety is a completely normal emotion in human beings, and its primary function is survival. All living beings, including animals, require a surveillance system to survive, and that normal anxiety is what fulfills that role in specific situations. It is that, it is normal that we are afraid when a real danger is presented. Our body is even designed to feel it under certain circumstances, obviously, to avoid fatal damage. For example, crossing a busy street, walking at night in a dangerous place or going into the woods, etc. It would be stupid not to feel fear in life and death situations.

However, sometimes it happens that all this incredible disaster prevention mechanism does not work as one would like, producing false alarms in the event of any danger. At this point we come to what an anxiety disorder is. This type of disorder is identified because they are the main elements that cause constant human suffering. In psychology it is called a clinical picture:

The main disorders that derive from anxiety are:

- panic disorders
- phobias
- Obsessive Compulsive Disorder also known as OCD
- chronic stress
- fears
- Chronic generalized anxiety

It should be noted that the symptoms of anxiety could also be caused directly or indirectly by specific conditions: such as some disease, or the consumption of drugs such as methamphetamine, cocaine , marijuana or diet drinks, as well as the consumption of certain drugs, medication hormonal etc.

Let's take a closer look at each of the disorders derived from anxiety below:

panic disorder:

— "I feel like I'm having a heart attack, and I think I'm going to die." Monica is a young primary school teacher who has suffered from anxiety attacks for 1 year. The first time he had a seizure he went to the ER because he thought he was having a heart attack. She never imagined that she had anxiety, much less did she think that the doctors would take so little importance to her supposed urgency. They only told her: "you have anxiety", and they prescribed a pill, a medication that at first took away her symptoms and left her a little sedated and sleepy, but after a couple of weeks she realized that the monster was still there. ..

I was always aware of his heart rate if it was racing. Despite the fact that before she was an athlete, Monica gradually stopped running because she was afraid that her heart would beat fast, and it was impossible for her not to notice it... She also began to distance herself from her partner little by little due to the fear of holding sexual intercourse, the same, because of the terror that dying of cardiac arrest caused him due to feeling the accelerated heartbeat that is normal in physical activity...

Panic disorder is identified by the intense fear of experiencing the entire chain of symptoms again in certain places or at specific times. A panic attack is an intense fear that usually occurs suddenly, and reaches its maximum intensity in a couple of minutes, maintaining a maximum of twelve. To call it a panic attack, it must be accompanied by at least 3 of the following elements:

- restlessness and anxiety
- Tachycardias ranging from 100 to 165 beats per minute
- Choking sensation (feeling of not being able to breathe)
- Unfocused chest tightness
- A choking sensation, inability to swallow saliva
- upset stomach, diarrhea
- Dizziness
- Unreality: feeling that you see everything in an unreal way as if you were dreaming it
- Depersonalization: feeling like you're not inside of the body, as if you were floating
- Almost uncontrollable anxiety and fear of going crazy, especially at night
- Fear of dying and that strange people will observe you in your nakedness in the morgue
- Numb jaw or tingling sensation in hands and feet
- Feeling chilly and uncontrollable shaking

Panic disorder is defined by specialists as the fear of fear or the phobia of fear. In essence, the person who suffers from it is terrified that simple harmless symptoms will manifest as a potentially deadly sign, so by thinking and feeling that, they create a fear that overflows, generating all the pictures already described with Monica.

So remember the stage of a panic attack, the sensation is just an example, focus on the interpretation that is always the main point because everything is triggered:

<u>Sensation anxious interpretation</u>

D sharp odor in he chest	I'M DYING HELP
pain or discomfort in he chest	I COULD DIE I WON'T BE HAVING A HEART ATTACK
almost imperceptible pain in the chest area	WHAT IF I AM HAVING A HEART ATTACK
	I'M AFRAID IT COULD BE A
chest oppressed	BREATH...
	I'M AFRAID OF BEING OPERATED

These are usually the main ones, but they also tend to misinterpret vertigo as a sign that they've had a stroke, and it's only a matter of time before they pass out and become unconscious, and obviously the dizziness comes from hyperventilation. Crises or panic attacks are usually a very difficult problem to deal with, because it prevents you from enjoying life due to the constant fear that chains you to being afraid that they will appear in the least expected places. And the fear of being branded crazy.

Agoraphobia:

pepe case

— "I don't want to go looking for a job, I feel like I'm going to faint." Pepe started having panic attacks two years ago... at first his greatest terror was falling due to dizziness and bleeding to death. As they became stronger and more periodical, he realized that there were certain places where the monster was unleashed. And these places were where there were many people in places such as: department stores, cinema, schools, etc. At first he tried to avoid hours when there were a lot of people because that way he was calmer... then the disorder escalated to the point of being unable to go to places like this alone. This disorder affected him so much that he lost his job as a teacher at a university, due to the fear of speaking in large groups and what they will say. As simple as getting around on the bus, it was impossible for him because every time he got off he was terrified that they would look at him as his pants fit in the back, or they would look at him in profile, especially the girls. Unfortunately, it can happen that we "solve" fear radically, avoiding those places where we get the crisis. The bad thing about this is that this avoidance can trigger other problems until reaching a disorder called chronic agoraphobia.

People who have this disorder tend to avoid many situations from those already mentioned to the unthinkable. For example, going to look for work, walking through heights, going in elevators, traveling in planes, trucks, etc. For the agoraphobic any of these situations before their perception is a life or death threatening situation.

It should be noted that agoraphobia is not always directly related to panic attack disorder. What maintains this disorder in itself is avoiding those kinds of places that cause fear. Consequently, anxiety crises are caused by going to such places... What happens is that in those particular places there are favorable circumstances for the chain of symptoms that trigger the panic, nervous crisis, etc. to begin. All the symptoms are harmless, but in the mind of the person in question the catastrophic interpretation occurs. Therefore, avoiding those places will be counterproductive because you will become involved in your circle of security to the point of totally isolating yourself from many things that you used to enjoy. It is sad, but in many cases their lives end without having enjoyed it due to fear of this disorder.

Social phobia:

— "I am only able to look for jobs where I can be alone or there are no women." Manuel.

There are many like him... There are people who spend months without leaving home, others who feel a terrible fear of only going to the center of the city by bus for fear of being looked at... others fear situations or jobs where they are in contact with people. They hate working in groups because of what they will say, and if they make a mistake while working, they suffer to a great extent from being pointed out to such a degree that many get depressed for days by a simple pointing out of an error... The person with social phobia is very hard on himself in your mind. Repeat the same scene over and over again. For example, if someone corrected them for a mistake in public, they will exaggerate a thousand times in their mind, self-flagellation. The person with social phobia does not fear the person himself, but fears judgments, what they will say, criticism, looks... Opinions regarding his person, his clothing, his speech, his thoughts... it is that is why they are usually silent if they work in any case. It is one of the disorders that is least taken into account in companies. Without imagining that many of the resignations around the world in the first weeks are due to social phobia.

This disorder is essentially an anxiety disorder that goes unnoticed by most. Even for the person who suffers from it many times. Usually the social phobic tends to blame his character and the very stressful situation he lives. That is why many social phobes will never know love... they fear a criticism of a no. For example, a guy hitting on a girl is unthinkable. We must be very clear that shyness is not the same as having a social phobia. Although, the shy person may experience anxiety, but he does not confine him at home or in general situations. In other words, it does not invalidate it to be your normal life. A person with a phobia can suffer economic and love crises due to their simple condition. I have known people who lasted up to 10 years without a job due to the fear of being in situations like this.

The shy individual does not incapacitate his personality. It's not as open, but it doesn't prevent you from performing in work areas either. Perhaps you are not looking for public jobs such as: bars, restaurants, but you do well in offices, factories, etc. On the other hand, for the person who suffers from social phobia, everything is very complicated in situations even with few people, such as: looking for a girlfriend, conversations in groups, eating in public, defending oneself in verbal situations, raising one's voice, looking for a job, etc. These simple situations that for the majority are normal for these people are hell, since they cause them when they are exposed: colitis, diarrhea, headaches, muscle aches, dry mouth, palpitations... And they end once they return to their bubble. security (comfort zone). It is very common for people with phobias to fear that other people will find out about their problem. That's why they try not to sweat, turn red or tremble to avoid more insecurities and shame in their perception.

In fact, I met a person who I omit his name out of respect, who had a postgraduate degree in business administration, but because he had social phobia, he decided to get a night job as a watchman in a pantheon. The biggest dream I had told me; it was to find a job in a lighthouse at sea alone... it was his most cherished dream. It is not unusual for social phobes to suffer from panic attacks, although it is not a general rule. The solution that most adopt to avoid facing these intense discomforts are three options: escape from these scenarios, avoid them or hide them, even if it entails all the symptoms already described in secret. Unfortunately, a large number of these people to control their symptoms resort to drugs, tranquilizers or substances to stay calm in social contexts.

Specific phobias:

They are characterized by illogical and exaggerated fears in certain situations (I underline the illogical and exaggerated) before being exposed to feared environments or contexts. There are several kinds of phobias:

- **The environmental:** usually fear of heights, sea, rivers, electricity, rain everything that is found in nature in an inanimate way.
- **Animal** : they are usually excessive fears of certain animals, insects, arachnids, birds, etc.
- **To the blood:** fear of infecting all kinds of pathogens and viruses such as: HIV, hepatitis, gonorrhea, etc.
- **Situations of daily life:** fear of driving due to a crash, going on a trip for fear of accidents, etc.

It has been proven that without a correct guide to manage this type of fear in the long run, the person could acquire a chronic degenerative disease of an organic type.

Obsessive-compulsive disorder :

The particular thing about this disorder derived from generalized anxiety is precisely the obsession about a certain thing or situation. Obsessions are those thoughts or images that suddenly appear outside of us. And usually they are almost uncontrollable and involuntary. It is normal that those who do not suffer from it do not have the slightest idea of the anguish that is felt, and therefore they consider themselves crazy. For example, there are people who have thoughts in the form of images where they see themselves murdering their wife or family member and fear that at a certain moment they will lose control in reality. Most agree that the more they struggle to get rid of those thoughts; stronger they get. Some run with all their might down the street, others shake their heads to get rid of those thoughts, others scratch themselves and some bite themselves and make small cuts. There are different types of obsessions that are divided into several categories such as:

- **The aggressive:** fear of committing a crime when those images and thoughts come to mind. They become worse if you have a loved one in front of you. Fear of blaspheming against God, and saying bad words, fear of committing suicide. Etc.
- **Or become obsessed with dirt:** exaggerated concern for fear of catching viruses, bacteria or harmful

substances. Fear of contracting a sexual disease. As an additional fact, many who suffer from these phobias go their entire lives without having sex or even giving a hug.

- **Sexual obsessions:** Extreme fear of sex or morbid fixations on the opposite sex. Fear of becoming a homosexual, or a pedophile. Flood of atypical and strange sexual thoughts. Sex distortion. Recurring thoughts around him. Etc.

- Another type of fear that occurs is mixed; like terror of waking up one day and not being able to speak, remember, or you think you've gone crazy and you take out a sum like 2 plus 2 to see if it makes sense and check with yourself if you've really gone crazy. Obsession to perfection. Etc.

Post Traumatic Stress Disorder:

Everyone at some point in life will have to go through some tragic event; from accidents, rapes, kidnappings and cruelty of other people. Among some other unpleasant situations that you can imagine. When we have been between life and death, or involved in extremely shocking negative situations, it is what is called post-traumatic stress. It basically consists of re-experiencing such an event in the form of repetitive nightmares, nocturnal or daytime memories, indirectly or directly by thought association. Any idea or thing that reminds us of such a situation tends to trigger an altered state of mind and obviously anxiety. For example, going through a certain street that reminds us of where a relative was murdered. People who experience this condition tend to avoid everything that evokes these events. Therefore, they do everything possible not to talk or think about it, avoiding all contact and activities or work that may bring back bad memories. A large percentage of people who have marked PTSD have moderate to severe depression. And in many cases those who do not receive treatment can end their lives. This disorder can last for weeks, months, and even years.

Generalized anxiety:

The famous generalized anxiety is the one that is not focused on any context or scenario that we mentioned above. For example, in panic disorders, recurring crises and situations are feared, places where the famous attack could occur. In social phobias; the fear of social situations and what people will say. In specific phobias, the fear of certain contexts, situations already mentioned such as flying, walking in heights or being near deep places of water. obsessive compulsive disorder; fear of germs, profanity , to name a few. And the post-traumatic; the memories or lived events of life or death or where there were psychological traumas. But in generalized anxiety disorder there is not that fear of a certain thing or specific issue, but you fear everything at the same time. Individuals who have generalized anxiety are prone to excessive worry out of the blue. As if they were always worried about something as simple as work, study, partner, fear of having an accident. They find it impossible to stop worrying about simple day-to-day things. And obviously, being like this for a long time causes the symptoms that we have already mentioned to arise; from palpitations to difficulties sleeping and terrible anguish .

The mechanisms of generalized anxiety

The first chapter basically consisted of knowing the different ways that anxiety has to manifest itself. In this section we will take a closer look at the mechanism. In order to deal with it, the first thing we have to do is identify the causes - factors that directly or indirectly intervene in why a person can experience anxiety in circumstances in which other human beings do not usually present it.

Specialists differentiate four major causes or factors to understand the mechanism of this disorder.

1) The contexts - the circumstances - the situations that release the anxiety response chain

2) At the physiological level in a certain determined circumstance

3) How do we respond to anxiety?

4) Consequences to the symptomatology

➡➡➡**Circumstance physiological response anxious response consequences or actions**

Next, let's take a deeper look at the things you need to be aware of to overcome this disorder.

Anxiety triggers

These variants may depend on each person, but for the most part they are the main ones that occur, although they are not directly related to any disorder:

- go to crowded places
- Go by elevator or lift
- Stay in a line or save our turn
- speak in front of many people
- Being watched by a group of people
- Receiving criticism intensifies if there are several at the same time
- Conversing with an attractive or authoritative person
- Eating or drinking in crowded places
- Travel by airplane
- see blood or wounds
- make important decisions
- Go to job interviews
- think ahead
- think about death
- For not being happy with their appearance (there are many people who simply do not look good in their pants or a certain item of clothing, etc.

All this does not mean that fearing something in particular forces us to fear other directly or indirectly related situations. For example, there are people who find it scary to speak in front of a large group of people, but they are not afraid of proposing to a girl. Here the point is that to determine the severity of any generalized anxiety disorder, it does not matter how many situations the person fears, but rather how much the feeling of anxiety affects their life. It makes it difficult for you at work, at a work, personal, social level, etc.

Perhaps you who read this book think that there is no situation that causes you anxiety and you are right. There are people who do not have any particular situation as their cause. In psychology, it is preferred to use stimuli because it is easier to include thoughts, emotions, memories, sensations as causes of anxiety. An example is that we do not fear any situation in particular, but if we fear that they will look at us... that thought of fear of being looked at nervously produces anxiety.

Responses that anxiety initiates in the different disorders that we already mentioned when they occur. Important to know:

Active physiological response:

- palpitations
- feeling of oppression
- Shortness of breath
- Blushing (redness on the face)
- Diarrhea. Etc.

Cognitive responses:

- Memories of a horrible accident
- rape or abuse or remember the face of the criminals
- Blasphemous thoughts towards your parents or God
- Recurring doubts about sexual orientation
- Doubts after a few seconds that he has left the place about whether the doors, windows, gas taps have been

closed properly, washed his hands well, etc.

- Perception of oneself as strange or distant from reality
- Violent images or aggressive content in the mind

Physiological motor responses:

- hand tremor for minutes
- Difficulty speaking stuttering
- Weakness in the legs and hands feeling faint

Our physiology in situations

Suffering from anxiety is somehow inherited to some extent. It should be noted that we do not inherit a specific disorder, but we do inherit that certain physiological receptivity to more easily suffer tachycardia, muscle tension, among all the symptoms already described. By having this availability to react to certain circumstances than other individuals, it is easier to learn alarm reactions to certain contexts than is normal for others. Therefore, this genetic receptibility does not produce anxiety.

Cognitive symptoms: cognitive symptoms are all those recurring images and thoughts that are triggered in our minds when we are in an anxious picture, that is, those thoughts that automatically come to mind in a certain situation.

In the following table you can see in general the cognitive symptomatology

Anxiety widespread	**symptomatology cognitive**
panic disorder	the answer Physiological is: Tachycardias chills , tremor: and your symptoms cognitive are: **thinking** If I faint , if I die for an attack cardiac , and if ...
_	**Thoughts :**
Agoraphobia	**And if I die in the movies... if I fall during the interview in front of the rest... if I go to the bathroom in front of the girl I like...**
phobias specific	**think :** "And if he gives me the cancer ." "the elevator could spoil ." And if I get hit by a car
Disorder obsessive compulsive (OCD)	Images mental or thoughts recurring : Although You just saw that you closed the gas tap , you come back over and over time to check _ and you are not nice until someone further tea say this closed
social phobia	**Thoughts :** -I'm sure when it's my turn I'll make it terrible ' -They are giving account that I am Turning red and they'll say I'm weak and scared -What will they think? when they greet me and I have my sticky hand by he fear that I feel
Disorder by stress post traumatic -	**think :** think again about events past like : Never i will do it again happy And if they kidnap me other time ... if they kill me

Fear and anxiety present themselves physiologically through dozens of symptoms, such as muscle tension, tachycardia, high breaths, vomiting, nausea, oral dryness, sweating, tremors, chills per minute, hot flashes, insomnia, headaches, severe neck pain that sometimes they are confused with cervical problems, chronic to moderate fatigue, cutting diarrhea. Fortunately all these symptoms do not appear suddenly but imagine: it would be terrible. Unfortunately, having all these symptoms in certain stages of anxiety can give rise to different alterations in our health such as the famous irritable bowel, colitis, constipation, bruxism. High breathing - hyperventilation plays an important role in a panic disorder. For example, sometimes when there is an increase in respirations in a short time, this increase in oxygen at the blood level in many people causes the aforementioned chain of symptoms. And precisely those symptoms, such as dizziness, a strange sensation, are normally misinterpreted as a sudden heart attack or imminent madness. And then the panic attacks come for weeks.

Specialists agree that at least 75% of people will suffer from at least one panic disorder in their entire lives. As you can see in the box above, many symptoms, if not all, are repeated in almost all disorders. And that is because anxiety has a similar physiological manifestation in all anxiety disorders, although the situations and thoughts that cause said condition are different.

When we are anxious, most people notice the chain of symptoms in us less than we think. Particularly in those individuals who suffer from social phobia, and believe that everyone is noticing that they are super nervous in a certain situation, nothing is further from the truth. On the contrary, avoiding fleeing in those situations that scare us the most is an immovable symptom for the problem to continue. For this reason it is essential to learn to control - properly manage our thoughts and the flood of images that automatically assault our minds. Face in our daily life those situations that we usually avoid or flee; It's the last step we have to take to once and for all overcome this terrible monster disguised as a kitten.

You can see the main motor symptoms of anxiety grouped by anxiety disorders.

anxiety disorder _	symptomatology motorboat
panic disorder _	avoiding or escaping from situations in which you think you could have an anxiety attack . Avoid or stop doing activities that _ _ _ cause symptoms physiological feared (tachycardia , suffocation , oppression in he chest , etc.), for example : do sport or keep relations sexual .
Agoraphobia Disorder _	Avoiding or running away from situations stressful or fearful _
social phobia _	Avoid or flee from situations that are feared . difficulty speaking _ choking stutter . tremors visible hands or legs
The Phobias specific	avoiding or escaping from situations feared .
Disorder obsessive compulsive	Avoiding or escaping from situations you fear . wash hands, put object order _ things , check things excessively . _
Disorder by stress post traumatic	Avoiding or escaping from situations , people, or objects that remind of the situation traumatic _
anxiety disorder _ widespread	restlessness _ can appear as touching repetitive hair , nose , cracking _ the fingers , discomfort to remain sitting etc anger _ also can express themselves visibly to others (arguments , complaints , fights etc.).

The consequences of the anxiety response

Be it any direct manifestation of anxiety, it is logical that we want to reduce that annoying discomfort. However, the consequences of behavior play a very significant role in the way we act and maintain a picture of this condition:

- I have a panic attack at the cinema and I run out. When I leave, I feel relieved, I can breathe easier and my palpitations decrease.
- They ask me to come to the front of the class and present my point of view... I feel that some have already noticed it: that they thought of me, so little by little I begin to miss classes.
- I am terrified just thinking that my daughter has an accident, so I strongly forbid her to go out with her friends, thus reducing my feeling of anxiety.
- If I greet someone with HIV, I feel that I have to wash my hands repeatedly up to 7 times, when I do, I manage to get rid of that absurd idea that I won't get infected that way.

The enumeration could go on and on... but at the end of it all we would end up with the same thing, that the things we do based on a certain situation contain the essence of a neutral anxious problem. You might say at this point: what's wrong with running away if it makes me feel better? Well, it's a very good question, but since this informative guide aims to give you guidelines - teach you alternative behaviors to be able to at least take the first step to control your anxiety , obviously, it is vital to do those things that give us improvement. But the question is what kinds of things – actions – behaviors make us feel better. What matters even more is how long that improvement lasts... is it short-term or permanent?

The main problem with the behaviors that we gave as an example in the list above, is that only in the short term they give us the feeling of peace, but in the long term it will continue to be ineffective and detrimental to our quality of life, and let's see below for that:

- I have a panic attack at the cinema and I run out. When I leave, I feel relieved, but for a short time I can breathe easier and the palpitations decrease. In the long term, it will worsen and perhaps the person believes that the cinema causes such a crisis and considers that it is a dangerous place.
- If I greet someone with HIV, I feel that I have to wash my hands repeatedly up to 7 times, when I do, I manage to get rid of that absurd idea that I won't get infected that way. For short term. It is well known that the more time passes, the obsession can increase. I have known people who started washing their hands or washing a certain object for fear of getting x germs... At first they started washing 4 times and after a few years the OCD worsened and they washed up to 40 times at a time.

It is evident that the tranquility that causes us in the short term to flee or avoid situations that cause us anxiety, in the end is counterproductive in the long term for our quality of life.

Because we come to lose contact with reality in a certain way in all situations due to the threats that we feel are stalking us. When we run away from a certain situation, we believe that if we had been left feeling those annoying symptoms, anxiety would have continued to rise and rise to unsuspected levels. But the truth is that they are harmless if you face it. Avoiding a situation has a similar effect to fleeing, unfortunately it does not allow us to see what would have happened in such a situation that we fear, and so we end up imagining that the worst would have happened. The next time you present a similar scenario, you may think, and for what? It is a very personal answer, but if you do it to me, I would say, to not let time pass and enjoy those wonderful moments that you are letting slip away. Facing reality is the best thing you can do. Undoubtedly, confronting those situations that we fear is transcendental to overcome our fears and anxieties.

Anxiety and emotional chemistry

People suffering from anxiety are often triggered by chemicals directly or indirectly. In fact, most of the substances that we will see later can cause:

- Anxiety disorders or increasing them
- Aggravate disorders that you already had
- Or seemingly 'fix' anxious problems
- Chronify the problem

We will not delve into it because it is obvious, but the list that you will read below are the main substances that you should avoid if you feel that you have any problem derived from anxiety

- Coffee, cocoa and colas: because they contain very high levels of caffeine that favor all the anxious symptoms, although it is difficult to resist many of these drinks, it is advisable not to ingest them.
- Energy drinks: These drinks contain a kind of cocktail of vitamins, sugars, taurine, stimulants such as caffeine and guarana. Same effect as coffee, cola, cocoa, but 5 times stronger on anxiety.
- Alcohol, cocaine, amphetamines
- Cocaine can cause panic attacks
- Amphetamines and derivatives : These substances have a stimulating effect that can cause or aggravate anxiety disorders.
- Psychoactive drugs: anxiolytics

- antidepressants

It is recommended that you only and exclusively medicate for the most chronic and serious cases of anxiety, always under the control of a specialist. Anxiolytics are effective in some individuals, especially when it comes to managing acute symptoms. On the contrary, antidepressants have been shown to help chronic anxieties, however, medication is not the solution to the problem, it is only temporary, but it does help a lot when you are heading towards a definitive cure. Let's remember that anxiety is vital for our survival, but the important thing is to control it in the face of imaginary reactions or dangers, that is the definitive long-term solution.

3 guidelines to follow that you should take into account if you are not taking any type of medication yet:

- **If you still do not consume any medication** : Do not accept a treatment if it exclusively consists of the intake of medication. In certain cases it starts like this, because it is effective in the short term, but if you continue for a long time it will be very difficult for you to stop. Do not forget that our body will get used to anxiolytics, therefore it will become less and less effective for the symptoms and higher doses will be required.

- **If you are already taking medication prescribed by a specialist:**

Never stop taking your medication without your doctor's order. You should check yourself periodically to adjust your dose and even stop drug treatment if you have felt improvement. It has been scientifically proven in recent decades that cognitive behavioral class treatments have an efficacy similar to that of the best drugs and a much higher capacity to help you get out of anxiety.

- **If you are taking medication on your own:**

You should never take medication, since there are some drugs with an addictive power that is even higher than that of some illegal drugs. So immediately stop taking the medication you are taking and see your doctor. Never stop taking the medication on your own without prior notice from your specialist.

Now we have a broader notion of anxiety, its disorders, its general mechanism and its symptoms presented by those who suffer from it and some of the substances that chemistry affects our body, which in many cases contributes to making it worse. However, all this information, although it is very useful to give us an idea, is still very general to help us get out of our anxiety in a meaningful way. And it is precisely in the next chapter where we will discuss how to deal with it.

If you feel that you have generalized anxiety or have doubts even after reading this guide, my honest advice is that you go to a specialist such as a professional psychologist or psychotherapist; they will help you and diagnose you if you suffer from any disorder derived from the same GAD, and they will offer you available options that can help you get ahead. Reading this book can be of great help as a complement. In the following section we have selected a series of the most effective techniques proven for the type of anxiety you have. The techniques will be grouped into two aimed at two objectives:

- **Get a physical relaxation**
- **get mental relaxation**

A muscle relief or progressive muscle relaxation

Progressive relaxation basically consists of practicing a series of easy muscle tension and relaxation exercises. The main goal that we want to reach with these specific exercises, at the beginning is not so much to achieve a general muscular relaxation but to know how to differentiate the different states of muscular tension that we suffer. Usually most of us do not pay too much attention to the areas where there is more tension, and precisely that tension is what creates a lot of the feeling of physical discomfort.

How to carry out said relaxation

It is essential that you take into account that you will require discipline to carry them out, and at least 12 days for you to begin to feel a noticeable muscular improvement. This may not give you much encouragement when the medication gives you that relaxation immediately, in a certain way it is, but in the long run this technique will give you permanent well-being. And the benefits are enormous... once you know how to relax, you won't need to take any medication to feel good.

You can record these instructions with a voice or someone with a calm voice can give you the guidelines so that you can carry them out.

Make yourself as comfortable as possible. Try not to think about anything, you will only focus on your body. close your eyes and begin to concentrate on all those sensations that are going to appear in moments...

We'll start with your left arm. I want you to focus your attention solely on your left arm... try to clench your fist until you feel the tension that is produced in all your fingers and it runs through your entire forearm and reaches your shoulder... don't let go... keep that force sustained for 10 or 12 seconds until you can fully feel the tension... now release all that contained force in a sudden way. Now immediately focus on that feeling of relaxation that is now occurring in your hand and running down your forearm and part of your shoulder. I want you to focus solely on that. That you feel heaviness or lightness, maybe you feel a tingling or something warm... that's fine, don't worry, do you feel your arm is lazy? That is exactly the muscle relaxation that I was telling you about.

Again do the same as you did with your left hand, but now tense your right hand from shoulder to fist, hard enough that you feel some discomfort in your fingers. 10 seconds again and let go... feel that sensation as soon as you let go of your arm and hand, it should be completely limp.... Breathe again in the same way; soft and light without forcing it, the air should come out effortlessly ... inhale deeply and hold for 5 seconds and exhale. I want you to breathe with the lower part of both lungs slowly and without pressing you... you will see that little by little you will get used to it...

Perhaps you noticed that when you clenched your left or right fist, some areas of your body also contracted, including your other arm... it's normal at first. But watch out! It is vital that you concentrate so that only that area we want is tense. It is essential that we learn to relax the rest of the other parts of our body so as not to feel those tense sensations. We will learn that a little later.

We repeat now in our right fist, and we release the contained tension... I want you to repeat this exercise at least 3 times in each session, as slowly as possible... there is no hurry. You must know every sensation of your body. Just as you are relaxed with both arms and breathing plus your mind blank, we will move on to the next exercise.

Now we will focus on the muscles of our face only. Surely you already realized that it is somewhat more complicated, but as you practice you will improve. To do this, keep in mind that you must tense the area of the forehead, between the eyebrows, eyelids, nose , lips, cheekbones, jaw and obviously the tongue. Now we are going to start with the forehead, for that try to raise your eyebrows strongly... yes! raise them as high as you can and hold for 10 seconds... now release just as hard, you will feel some fatigue and some freedom in your face.

Now just tense your eyelids, squeeze them! you will feel a slight tension, release that force now... just your eyelids relax, you feel the relief, right? although a little tired... do it one more time and then let go...

Now tighten your eyelids. Squeeze them! Feel the gentle tension in your eyes... and release the tension. The eyelids relax, remain loose and hardly feel...

Now it is the turn between the eyebrows and the nose... you will feel hard between those two areas... now you feel a contained force, right? Let go, as soon as you do it you will notice how that area relaxes, only that area... you will feel the sensation of tension and relaxation in seconds. Do it again and release. Notice each sensation of squeezing, releasing, squeezing, releasing.

Squeeze your jaw, and the tongue that pushes against the palate. You should feel the force for 10 seconds in your jaw and tongue... Let go of your tongue... it remains relaxed , just like your jaw. Repeat the same exercise again.

At this time your entire face has relaxed, along with both arms, and your breathing is calm and relaxed.

Now it's time to relax your neck. To do it you can try to touch your chin to your chest or simply push your neck for 10 seconds. You feel the tension... it's rigid, hard. Now release the force in your neck... it is relaxed a little tired but relaxed. Repeat again. At this point I want you to notice all your attention on the feeling of well-being that is coming together. Fluid breathing without forcing, relaxed arms, face and now neck, and obviously the most important thing; your mind solely concentrated on these sensations on nothing else... I don't want you to think of anything other than here in your present.

To tense our shoulders we will try to make them backwards as if we wanted to play backwards from behind. You feel the tension... loose. Our back seems to relax. Repeat the exercise again, but now go ahead and relax. Feel each of those sensations...

Now squeeze your abdomen, as if you were going to do a sit-up. Squeeze it for 12 seconds and release, see how you felt the contained force! and now it is soft and relaxed again . Surely you have already noticed how pleasant it is to feel the sensation after being tensed...

Now I want you to tense your middle and lower back. Try to arch your back as if you wanted to push your stomach forward. Do it... feel the little tension... now let go. In the same way as the previous simple exercises you feel the relaxation... do it again, don't forget to focus on each pleasant sensation when you release the tension...

At this moment you already have fluid and relaxed breathing, not forced, oxygen enters and relaxes you... your thoughts are in the now, you don't think of anything other than those sensations that you had not paid attention to before... the breath continues very deep and you relax more and more.

Right now it is the turn of our left leg, to do so, forcefully tense your thigh from the buttock to the tip of the foot as if you were going to put the brake on the car. You see that the tension is felt... let go now... As you feel the area of the calf, the thigh, the foot relax... I want you to focus on each sensation of the whole leg, I want you to know each sensation that is perceived when you are tense and when you relax... I want you to become it do the same.... Release, and feel those relaxing sensations each time you contract and release . Now repeat the same, but with your right leg...

At this point your whole body is completely relaxed... your face, your neck, the shoulder area, your stomach, the back area, and obviously both legs... your breathing continues in harmony, calm and with such deep breaths without force; your energy is renewed and the tension in your body gradually goes away... and you realize that relaxation gives you a lot of peace and improvement... you have the right to that, we all have it, but for that you have to learn it...

Keep your eyes closed, don't open them... enjoy that relaxation in your mind anyway...

After at least 8 minutes like this you can get up. Do not get up abruptly, do it gently since in this muscle relaxation exercise you have made all your muscles loose without tension and you may feel unwell.

*I want to emphasize that this effective muscular exercise is widely used in the main therapeutic centers around the world. It is essential to put it into practice at least 2 times a day for approximately 10 to 15 minutes.

I recommend that you do it in a quiet place without interruptions, or much better in a place surrounded by nature, you will see that the results will be incredible. As with any other exercise, the quality in our relaxation will come the more we practice daily. Without a doubt, the best benefits of this exercise will come after a couple of weeks at most a month, as long as you do it at least twice a week.

If you record the previous exercise in audio, it is essential that you do it with a harmonic rhythm and intonation so that it is equally stimulating. If at first it is difficult for you to leave your mind blank, do not do it, do not force your thoughts, but you should focus on the exercise and the sensations you feel.

Those individuals who suffer from panic disorders should keep in mind that this type of exercise puts them more in tune with their physiological sensations; such as heartbeat, breathing etc. Precisely this can be frightening, but it is not, keep in mind that they are harmless. If you feel dizzy due to controlled breathing, don't do it so intensely. Remember gradually you will achieve a high level of concentration even with deep breathing.

There are other ways to relax our muscles, one of them is mild to moderate physical exercise. Next, we will see which are the best.

Best sports that can help you relax

- **The Yoga:** In the face of repeated anxiety pictures, it is advisable to practice this exercise. It is clinically proven that this practice helps to control breathing and achieve mental and physical peace, it also helps to obtain an adequate awareness of our body in addition to controlling emotions in a positive way.

- **Boxing – MMA:** It is very useful for severe anxiety pictures. Specialists from all over the world agree that boxing or MMA as a sport greatly alleviates anxious symptoms in addition to depression, because it supplies an enormous amount of happiness hormones such as endorphins, oxytocics, dopamine, serotonin., and therefore a positive and happy state of mind. In addition, it increases our self-esteem as we improve and make changes in our body.

- **Pilates:** Pilates practice is highly recommended for individuals suffering from panic attacks. It helps you control your body and master those urges plus it gives you a high level of ability to focus with practice. In addition, it makes you move better and without pain, which creates a chain of well-being. Remember that to be happy the first requirement is to feel physical well-being.

- For insomnia derived from anxiety, the best activities

you can do are all those of an aerobic nature, such as: walking, cycling, jogging, running, which incredibly improve blood circulation and our heart rate, relaxing our body and logically facilitating a better rest.

- **Team sports:** The difficulties we have to live with other people socially mainly reside in the lack of expressive skills and abilities and low self-esteem that we have. In cases of this nature, it is usually prescribed as support for therapy; the practice of sports in a group because it greatly improves our social skills. Among them are sports such as volleyball, soccer, basketball, etc. In this kind of sports it is vital to communicate with each other with simple messages that lead us to win as a team.

- **Swimming:** Swimming is a sport that is usually carried out individually, so it can be very useful for individuals who suffer from social phobias. It helps them little by little to immerse themselves in the social field.

Best foods to support your anxiety

Avocados: According to a study carried out by the University of Oxford in 2018, it revealed that foods with the highest level of vitamin B contribute to our physical well-being. According to this study, avocados are among the vegetables that contain the most this vitamin and are excellent stimulants for the release of neurotransmitters such as dopamine and exotoxin that have a positive emotional impact on our entire body.

Spinach : Another experiment carried out by the Broad Institute of MIT - United States. It revealed in mice that diets low in magnesium directly increased behaviors derived from anxiety, hence the importance of consuming foods with the highest magnesium content, such as: whole wheat, quinoa, and all kinds of almonds and peanuts.

Salmon : Research carried out in 2010 indicates that fatty amino acids such as omega 3 and its derivatives can significantly help against anxiety, since it impacts brain chemistry. Salmon or different varieties of fish are recommended at least two to three times a week as it greatly benefits to calm anxiety and insomnia.

Asparagus : This vegetable is perhaps one of the vegetables with the most studies proven to combat anxiety disorders. Such is its effectiveness that even the Japanese government approved the use of this vegetable extract in beverages as a supplement against anxiety.

Fruits with more Antioxidants: It has already been shown for years that having high levels of anxiety is directly related to very low antioxidant levels. We can control such anxiety by consuming foods rich in antioxidants, such as: nopales, lemons, garlic, beans, and all kinds of berries (strawberries, blackberries, red cranberries, broccoli, avocados. And all green fruits.

Almonds and nuts: One of those kinds of fruits to help us against this disorder, is to consume almonds and nuts every day due to their high contribution of vitamins B2, E and C, also helping to strengthen your immune system in cases of stress caused by the symptomatology of the tag.

Oatmeal and dark chocolate: It is a combined superfood and contains all the elements to induce calm in the body. In addition to lowering anxiety in minutes at least temporarily.

One of the tricks that usually work for anxiety, especially if you suffer from anxiety insomnia; It is a glass of hot milk with a levanta and linden tea, due to the ideal mixture of sedative properties.

Turkey : although it may seem incredible, turkey contains amino acid tryptophan in charge of helping fatigue and muscle relaxation, especially when you are tense due to the same disorder.

Sauerkraut. Among the best foods to combat anxiety we find those rich in probiotics such as sauerkraut or pickles or kefir.

Oysters: due to their very high level of zinc This mollusk is rich in vitamin B12, which is why they could help reduce pressure in the brain, according to a study published in the journal *Neurology*[1] *scientist* . Additionally, oysters have omega-3 fatty acids, a lack of which has been linked to increased risk of suicide and depression [2]. and anxiety

---

1.   *https://n.neurology.org/content/77/13/1276*

2.   https://www.ncbi.nlm.nih.gov/pmc/articles/PMC533861/

Techniques most used to reduce fears and anxiety

Autogenic relaxation: It is a psychotherapeutic technique that consists of the passive concentration of physiological sensations. This technique is based exclusively on all the sensations that are produced in our body based on stimuli with our voice. The purpose is to achieve total deep relaxation and lower stress and anxiety. The basis of this technique lies in 6 simple exercises that produce in the body that makes it feel in different states such as; warm, relaxed or heavy. In all the exercises the imagination and specific ways of speaking are used to objectively bring our body to that state of consciousness. I want you to record the following exercise in a sweet and calm voice, and then try to make it as comfortable as possible by lying in a chair that is comfortable for you. Example:

Start with a deep breath, but slow and calm, your exhalation being twice what you breathe... example. Breathe in for 5 seconds to the bottom, then exhale for 10 seconds slowly until you empty your lungs...inhale again, but slower something deep for 5 seconds, close your eyes and as you exhale hold them for 10 seconds, ok, inhale again now 6 seconds ... remember it will be twice the amount of exhalation ... your closed eyes continue to feel each sensation that the controlled breath produces. Now that you have done everything at least 2 times it is time to start...

now you will say to yourself: "my left arm will begin to feel heavy, "my left arm begins to weigh more and more". Concentrate on your arm and in the same way repeat this with all your extremities including face and neck.

Do not open your eyes, keep that concentration there... now start again with your right arm, but this time you will repeat it 6 times... my left arm will begin to feel more and more heaviness. Then continue with your whole body in the same way 6 times. Once finished, no matter how long it took you, repeat: "My breathing will begin to become more and more fluid... my stomach does not feel fear or discomfort... My heart begins to slow down... I feel calmer." Repeat it 5 times... once you've done that, breathe as deeply as possible without forcing your lungs... exhale for 10 seconds and while you empty them say: "all the stress is leaving, all the anxiety is leaving. Inhale... repeat positive messages to yourself... don't open your eyes yet, the affirmations combined with this technique are very powerful as they send messages to the subconscious, reprogramming it again. It is said that at least doing this technique for two months you will feel great results in your mentality.

Continue breathing... say: "I will heal, anxiety will leave my life just as it came... I am happy... breathe and inhale with that mental picture that you are happy, that you have already healed.

It is important that with each breath you take, you repeat that positive phrase... you must draw the scene in your mind as you exhale... it can be any phrase as long as they are positive. I recommend doing this technique once a day for at least 20 minutes. You will perceive great results if you do it with faith that you will be able to heal from your anxious pictures. There is nothing more powerful than a mind willing to change your mental patterns with positivity.

Mindfulness

Basically, this technique consists of having the ability to feel the present moment, both internally and externally while channeling and not paying attention to all those past anxieties, guilt, guilt, judgments, and negative thoughts. It can be used for anything, even for anxiety, in fact, the philosophy of mindful is that it is a way of living life.

I want you to do this exercise:

Find a peaceful place in your house... the ideal would be to practice it near a river, in the sea or surrounded by trees to enhance all the stimuli to your mind.

Position your body in a relaxed manner without lying down.

You can do them with your eyes open, but it is advisable to keep them closed since you get deeper into the emotions. Now I want you to focus on creating something with your mind right now, it can be a single positive thought, an object you love, a phrase you adore, or a place... focus on what you choose... focus, don't think just focus and feel the peace that gradually leads you to a deeper and deeper state of mind... focus on what you choose... don't create a story just focus on that, a thought, an object... veiled in your mind. If thoughts come out, let them flow, but don't worry about it, they will only fade away... just pay attention to that object or phrase you chose.

There are many exercises to learn, but if you have anxiety and need to calm it down quickly, I assure you that this basic mindfulness exercise will help you achieve it in minutes. You must do it at least twice a day for a minimum of 10 minutes. You will notice that once you master it in the depth of your concentration, the anxious symptomatology will reduce until it vanishes.

Meditation

To perform this exercise, just sit comfortably. Close your eyes, focus only on saying a mantra, that is, a powerful phrase in this case, you will say: I am not afraid, I am at peace... I love myself very much, I am healthy...

Put your hand on your stomach while you channel your own breath and repeat the series of sentences already mentioned, repeat them... ideally, repeat the phrases that you think are most positive for you at least 2 days in a row, in this way you will create a mental pattern that will gradually remove all the negativity that you have imposed on yourself due to anxious pictures over a long time. Everything that enters our conscious mind goes to the subconscious, so we'll be back to bringing our mind back to peak condition as we do more of these exercises.

If in any case you feel a flood of thoughts, don't try to throw them out, let them flow, but don't concentrate on them, it's easy, just don't give them importance. They will go alone. Keep concentrating on just keeping your eyes closed, breathing naturally and saying the powerful phrases or mantras: I am happy, I feel healthy, I feel complete peace... pay attention to your breathing... now that you are halfway through the exercise you won't say anything anymore. Instead of saying them you will say them with your mind and focus on your breathing. As you inhale and exhale I want you to pay attention to how your energy flows when you breathe in and when you release it.

When someone has anxiety due to the stress that comes with it, we usually breathe with the upper part of our lungs, so to lower that annoying feeling, let's do the following exercise:

Sit in a comfortable chair, put your hand on your belly and with the right on your chest...

Breathe through your nose for 5 seconds very, very slowly, so that your right hand on your chest begins to rise a little as a result of the inhaled air... now hold that oxygen for 5 seconds... then exhale through your mouth for another 5 seconds trying to get as much air out as you can while squeezing your abdomen hard. If at first the seconds are not comfortable for you, you can start at your own pace. The ideal is to slowly inhale for 15 seconds and hold for 15 seconds and then exhale for 15 seconds. Practice is the key, and this technique is extremely effective for panic attacks.

Now we are going to do another vital exercise, certainly it should be noted that not all people will be able to have great results, but there is a high percentage that has great results with this meditation technique.

Guided Imagination: It consists of imagining a landscape or scene in which you will vividly feel that you are there, obviously with the aim of relaxing from all those unpleasant sensations. It is one of the best techniques used to support cognitive therapies that are done against depression and fears. I want you to do it every day. Do it with all the faith that you will heal... I want you to make it as real as possible.

Just like the previous ones, find the best place where you can have peace, harmony and comfort. Close your eyes and imagine the most beautiful, calm and peaceful place on earth. Imagine it as realistic as your imagination allows, it is possible...!

Feel like in that place all your senses work one hundred percent... you can see the beauty of the place, you can feel the warm air that feels on your face. You can smell the precious vegetation that is around you, listen to the singing of the beautiful birds and some other sounds of animals while in the distance you see huge fields of wheat while the sunset amazes you... you feel and perceive textures, colors, smells, while you take with your hand a hazelnut flower.

Keep your eyes closed, it's time to walk through that wonderful place... imagine yourself starting to walk and feeling all those sensations... just as the place is wonderful and peaceful , you are equally at peace and in harmony with yourself... there is nothing wrong with you. bad in you, there is no anxiety: nothing only happiness and peace....

Keep walking like this and feeling all that range of sensations that your senses can give you and let any worries, negative thoughts or anxieties flow... little by little you will realize that by practicing this mental picture at least once before going to work or after returning, any anxiety you have will decrease incredibly.

Remedies against anxiety

Although natural remedies are not cures for anxiety, they can greatly benefit us to relax and sleep. These remedies are very useful, obviously as long as they are accompanied by everything we have mentioned in the previous sections. And of course with psychotherapies or following treatments prescribed by a specialist.

If you want to ditch chemical-containing drugs and want just as effective natural remedies, here is a list that might help you:

Valerian infusions

This plant has been used for thousands of years for many kinds of ailments and a few years ago it began to be prescribed even by conventional pediatricians. Recent studies have shown that valerian root and leaves have a direct effect on **gaba neurotransmitters** , which are the main inhibitory neurotransmitters, that is, they induce stress and anxiety to dissipate.

The recommended dose is two sachets in an infusion 1 hour before going to sleep.

Green tea infusions

Despite the fact that this herb is quite stimulating due to its active substances, studies have also shown that it has great benefits for anxiety due to the theanine responsible for giving muscle and brain relaxation. In addition to helping tachycardia and blood pressure, ideal for people who suffer from panic attacks at night.

Recommended dose : 1 sachet infused 30 minutes before going to sleep. Or in your case 100 milligrams of L- theanine supplement . Fortunately they do not contain side effects.

Lemon balm

It has been used for more than 500 years for insomnia, anxiety and nervous disorders. It has relaxing properties that act fast. The recommended dose is an infusion if it is moderate anxiety. You should not consume more than 2 infusions because it is very stimulating, especially at night.

licorice root

One of the best to calm our body in situations of great stress, added to its powerful properties to regulate blood glucose levels. In addition to stimulating the cranial and cerebrospinal zone, automatically giving mental and muscular calm after several minutes of consuming it. The recommended dose is 100 milligrams of boiled root per 2 cups of water. Only consume when anxious pictures appear.

kava

Used against nervousness and insomnia, it is ideal for people who suffer from generalized anxiety. Its effectiveness is already scientifically endorsed.

Recommended dose: two infusions at night, especially 40 minutes before going to sleep.

linden

tea is one of the most consumed extracts for anxiety and fear pictures . Although not as potent as valerian, in combination it can be extremely effective. The dose is 3 sachets only when you have trouble relaxing before going to sleep or in the afternoon.

Passionflower

This infusion acts as an anxiolytic and is a calming and relaxing that comes from the passion flower . It was used by the Aztec and Mayan empire hundreds of years ago for its powerful analgesic and sedative effects in stressful situations. It is also used in cases of moderate depression because it produces feelings of euphoria and liveliness. In the same way it is used throughout the world in naturist centers as an ally against insomnia, anxiety and tachycardia. The ideal dose is an infusion if you present the symptoms.

skullcap

Skullcap is a very effective plant for people who suffer from anxiety and nervousness accompanied by muscle tension. It can be taken in tea. The dose 2 sachets in infusion. You can find it in health food stores.

Chamomile

Chamomile is a widely consumed infusion that has not only beneficial properties for digestion. This plant has anxiolytic properties and helps fight and reduce nervousness, at least that's what a study from Oxford University carried out in 2014 with 6,500 volunteers indicates.

Hypericum

This plant has great benefits , mainly to balance neurotransmitters, which has a direct impact on our mood. The ideal dose is two infusions before going to sleep.

arctic root

This plant favors the increase in the activity of serotonin, norepinephrine and dopamine, the neurotransmitters of happiness, so that immediately after taking the infusion you will feel unparalleled relaxation and well-being.

Hop

Bitter in taste, it is well known for its effectiveness in treating anxiety, nervousness, stress, and insomnia. It is used all over the world and does not present caring side effects, but it is only recommended to consume it if you suffer from anxiety. The dose only two infusions.

Ashwagandha Tea : It has a very pleasant flavor and directly combats anxious symptoms, two to 3 sachets a day if you suffer from chronic anxiety. It brings relaxation within 30 minutes of consuming it.

Luisa grass : ideal for mentally depressed people, it helps to calm moderate nerves. The dose used is usually two sachets before going to sleep. It is not advisable for pregnant or lactating women.

Tips that can help you face and overcome your fears

Do not run away from fears: not to say all, but most people who suffer from fears regularly always try to distract themselves so as not to focus on the problem, unfortunately most of the time it is temporary. Fortunately, and it is the best method to achieve it, if instead of running away from our fears we confront them for 10 minutes daily, little by little we will create a new brain pattern and we will stop fearing it, obviously there are thousands of fears, but in general it works almost for everyone. all. For example, if you have social phobia, the best way to get out of that fear is to expose yourself to situations with people. Exposure is the most effective method, and yes! It is repetitive, but there is no magic to get out of a fear if we do not confront it directly. Most psychotherapists use exposure therapies to treat phobias...

Expose yourself to that fear for at least 10 minutes a day, wherever it originates: thought, animal, situation, and you will see that little by little you will be able to get out of it. Nothing will happen to you when you expose yourself. It is our mind that makes us believe wrongly. We shouldn't care what they say either, maybe you think yes, but it's a horrible feeling to expose yourself and... If I understand, I go through it the same way... but believe me, once you expose yourself day after day to that feeling it will begin to fade little by little and when you least expect it you will say: that all that you felt a month, 2 months, 4, and 8 months ago was extremely ridiculous and illogical. Dare yourself!

Giving our fears an affectionate name: giving a name to all the fears we have can help us stop seeing them as dangerous and we will begin to accept them, and that is the first step to defeating them.

Becoming friends with them: it is difficult at first, but seeing them as friends, instead of threats, is essential to begin to take control over ourselves. For example, I was afraid that night would come for fear of not being able to sleep, well, I spent years like this until I started using this: first I exposed that fear, then I gave it a friendly name, and then made it my friend... little by little I began to lose that fear to the point of now looking at the past and laughing, obviously everyone lives their fears in a different way, and when they are in their moment, one does not look at them like that. But if you apply it, it could work amazingly for you.

Share your fears: When we were kids we used to tell dad our fears and somehow we felt calmer. Just like before, you can do it with someone who will listen to you and whom you trust. It is essential to go to an equal psychologist to treat your fears if you wish.

Require fear to remain: when this technique is applied so simple to do by all means that our fears stay, contrary to do the opposite; they leave. For this method to work, it is vital that when we suddenly feel fear, we concentrate on doing just this, retaining that fear as much as possible, especially in panic attacks, and when you least expect it, it will go away.

The essence of this book lies in giving synthesized information on anxiety about your problem and a timely explanation. Based on this information and depending on how anxiety arrived or develops in you, you should analyze whether to follow the guidelines mentioned in the book or see a specialist. Beyond the fact that the book can add value and make you feel better, my recommendation is that you go to a certified specialist as soon as possible.

The techniques and methods mentioned in this guide have a proven scientific basis. If this book has helped you feel even a slight improvement, the job is done and the credit is entirely yours. Remember, there is no magic to eliminate anxiety from one day to the next, but you can get rid of it if you put everything on your part.

I know it's hard to put everything this guide mentions into practice, but believe me, if you try; I know that it will be able to help you a lot because I myself have tried everything that is embodied here and they have given me amazing results. But regardless of this book, I reiterate, it is extremely vital that you receive a diagnosis to effectively and unambiguously determine the origin of your condition, and in this way it will be easier to find the right treatment for you. In good time, I hope this manual is of great help and you recover from that kitten dressed as a monster. Thank you so much.